SHARING OUR THOUGHTS

A Biblically Based
Parent and Child Journal

Written by Andrea Thorpe

Printed in the United States of America

ISBN 978-1-7324744-0-6

For Dad.
I miss you.

Contents

Introduction

Children are a heritage from the Lord, offspring a reward from him.
(Psalm 127:3)

I remember the first time I held each one of my three daughters. I remember staring into beautiful, brown, long lashed eyes. I remember the feel of their tiny fingers grasping mine. I remember shedding joyful tears that sprung from a thankful heart. I remember sitting in my hospital bed praying over each girl and asking God to give me wisdom in my mothering. And, I remember my own mother telling me to cherish this special time and warning me that the years would pass quickly.

As usual, my mother was right. The days of nursing, diapering, first teeth, first words, and first steps are just a memory. My trio is growing quickly, and the girls are on their way to becoming young women. Because the years are fleeting, I do my best to enjoy the "right now" moments with my daughters. I'm working to create and preserve memories we'll all look upon with fondness in the years to come.

One of the ways I created memories was through journaling. The concept was a simple one. I opened a blank journal and wrote a note to my daughter. Then, I left the journal in her room and waited for her to write back to me. She wrote a note of response and left the journal in my bedroom. We filled the pages with memories as we continued to pass the journal back and forth.

The journal I shared with my daughter turned out to be a precious gift for both of us. As I look back on our silly, sentimental, and serious notes, I remember our ups and downs, our celebrations, and our slip ups. I fondly recall the knock-knock jokes we shared and the questions we asked one another. I smile as I flip the pages and see the scriptures and words of encouragement we wrote. Journaling became a wonderful way to help my daughter and me maintain a positive relationship.

That single journal, started several years ago, marked the start of this project. I wanted to create an attractive, official, and lasting journal to share with others and I wanted it to include Biblical wisdom as well. *Sharing Our Thoughts* includes ten chapters based upon ten interesting themes. Each chapter includes an anecdotal introduction with Biblical content and a set of thought provoking questions for both parent and child. Because spiritual growth and communication are an important part of the parent and child relationship, each chapter also includes space for prayer requests and additional thoughts.

I hope *Sharing Our Thoughts* encourages you to create written memories and serves as a springboard for future discussions. I have prayed that your relationship will grow stronger as you write and share with one another. May the completed journal serve as a precious memento for years to come.

Journaling Guidelines

Pray for one another. One of the best ways to show love to others is by praying for them. Pray as you write journal responses and pray as you read journal responses. Ask God to speak to you and provide insight about your partner. Pray for God to bless and strengthen your relationship as you complete the journal.

Keep the contents of the journal private. Protect this journal. Writing down personal thoughts, ideas, dreams, and concerns takes courage and makes people vulnerable. Do not leave the journal in a place where others can open it up and read its private and personal contents. If there is something within the journal you wish to share with another person, be sure to get permission before doing so.

Do not rush to complete the journal. Take your time as you read the chapters and complete the entries. This journal does not include dates or time constraints, so move through the pages at a pace that works for you and your partner. Whether you journal once a week or a few times per week, take the time to provide detailed and thought filled responses.

Do not focus on spelling, mechanics, and grammar. Journaling is not meant to be a chore or an additional schooling activity. Do not sabotage your connection efforts by nitpicking over writing errors. Doing so may drain self-confidence and hinder your partner's desire to respond. Focusing on errors may also thwart creative thinking and strip away the fun of journaling.

Carry on conversation outside the journal. This journal is intended to be one of the many steps in the parent/child journey. The reading and writing are meant to foster dialogue. Talk about what you've read and written. Ask additional questions and follow up on the prayer requests shared. Use what you learn to spark future discussion.

Getting to Know You Even Better

Let's begin this journaling journey by answering some fun questions! This activity is intended to help you learn something new about one another. Read each question carefully and respond honestly, but use only <u>one word</u> to answer each question.

	Parent	Child
What is one word that describes you?		
What is something that scares you?		
What would your dream job be?		
What is your favorite color?		
Who is your best friend?		
What is your favorite beverage?		
Where is a place you'd like to visit?		
What is something that makes you laugh?		
What smell do you enjoy?		
What would you buy if you had $1,000?		
Who is your biggest fan?		
What is your most prized possession?		
What is something you do well?		
What makes you sad?		
Which season do you like best?		
What is something you want to learn?		
What is your favorite room at home?		
What is your nickname?		
What holiday do you like best?		
What is something you collect?		
What Olympic sport would you like to try?		

1. Wonderfully Made: You

We have nineteen mirrors of various sizes hanging throughout our house. It's nearly impossible for us to enter or leave a room without seeing ourselves. Sometimes we catch unintentional glimpses of ourselves as we rush out the door and head to soccer practice. At other times, we hang out in front of a mirror for several minutes as we style our hair. You can't hide in our house. Mirrors are everywhere!

Think about the last time you took a good look into a mirror. How did you feel about what you saw? Perhaps your reflection made you feel happy and gave you a boost of confidence. Maybe you were disappointed by your reflection and your confidence level dropped. Let me tell you something important. Your appearance does not determine your self-worth.

In Genesis 1:27, the Bible tells us something quite remarkable. We learn we are made in the image of God. We should be pleased with our reflections because they are reflections of God Himself. Later, in Psalm 139:14, the Bible tells us how we should respond to what we see in the mirror. "I praise you because I am fearfully and wonderfully made; your works are wonderful, I know that full well." The words *wonderfully made* describe you. Yes, YOU!

David, the talented musician, brave warrior, and mighty king of Israel wrote those words. And when he wrote them, David wasn't talking about flowers, birds, or trees. He was talking about human beings, the people God made. God, The Great Creator, intentionally designed and created each one of us with a divine purpose. God carefully chose our hair color, skin color, body shape, birth order, and personality, as well as our other characteristics.

God didn't make a single error when creating you or me! Each one of us is a beautiful and unique creation meant to bring God glory as we do His will. You are wonderfully made! Take a few moments to read Psalm 139:13-18 and then respond to these questions during your journaling time.

Parent Journal: You

1. When you look into a mirror do you like what you see? Why or why not?

2. Which relative do people say you look or act like? Do you agree or disagree?

3. What is one talent God has given you? How can you use this talent to bless others?

Parent Journal: You

4.   What do you like most about yourself? Why?

5.   Is there a story behind your name? Tell the story.

6.   Do you like your name? Why or why not?

Parent Journal: You

Prayer Requests:

I just want to say...

Child Journal: You

1. When you look into a mirror do you like what you see? Why or why not?

2. Which relative do people say you look or act like? Do you agree or disagree?

3. What is one talent God has given you? How can you use this talent to bless others?

Child Journal: You

4. What do you like most about yourself? Why?

5. Is there a story behind your name? Tell the story.

6. Do you like your name? Why or why not?

Child Journal: You

Prayer Requests:

I just want to say...

2. Never Alone: Friendship

My kids love spending time with their friends. Whenever they meet up with their besties, I know everyone is going to have a blast. Sometimes the kids choose to go out and do something entertaining, like watch a movie or skate at the rink. At other times, the kids prefer to hang out at someone's house, where they can put their feet up on the couch, eat snacks, and chat about whatever comes to mind. They know that friendship is one of life's greatest joys.

Jesus lived for about thirty-three years and while here, He enjoyed spending time with friends as well. His closest friends were a group of twelve men, better known as disciples. Jesus ate meals with the disciples and talked about life's most important matters with them. He led the disciples in ministry and prayed with them regularly. At times, Jesus even cried with the disciples. The disciples' lives were forever changed because of their friendship with Jesus.

Because relationships are important to God, friendships are important to God. He knew we would need healthy, strong, and meaningful relationships throughout our lives, so He created friendship as a way to provide us with company, comfort, and joy. God also created friendship so we would be able to give and receive help and encouragement.

In Ecclesiastes 4:9-10, Solomon, the son of King David and the wisest man who ever lived, tells us about the benefits of friendship. "Two are better than one, because they have a good return for their labor: if either of them falls down, one can help the other up. But pity anyone who falls and has no one to help them up." God expects friends to love, support, and care for one another.

Our lives would be much different if we had to go through life alone. But because of God's generosity, we don't have to. We've been given the gift of friendship. Read I Samuel 20 to learn about the friendship between Jonathan and David. Afterward, think about the meaning of friendship and respond to the following journal questions.

.

Parent Journal: Friendship

1. Think about your first friend. Who was it and how did you meet?

2. Describe a time when a friend encouraged you.

3. Has a good friend ever moved away? How did you deal with it?

Parent Journal: Friendship

4. Is it hard or easy for you to make friends? Why?

5. What is one thing you can do to become a better friend?

6. What is a trait you look for in a friend? Why is this trait important to you?

Parent Journal: Friendship

Prayer Requests:

I just want to say...

Child Journal: Friendship

1. Think about your first friend. Who was it and how did you meet?

2. Describe a time when a friend encouraged you.

3. Has a good friend ever moved away? How did you deal with it?

Child Journal: Friendship

4. Is it hard or easy for you to make friends? Why?

5. What is one thing you can do to become a better friend?

6. What is a trait you look for in a friend? Why is this trait important to you?

Child Journal: Friendship

Prayer Requests:

I just want to say...

3. Fight or Flight: Fear

When I was about seven years old, I had a frightening experience while on family vacation. I had been splashing around in the hotel's large outdoor pool, but soon became bored. I was feeling adventurous, so I decided to try something I'd never done before. I bravely strode over to the pool slide and climbed the rungs all the way to the top. I let out a triumphant shout and hurled myself down the steep slide. I zoomed down the slippery slope and screamed with joy the whole way down. Then, I plunged into the deep water, mouth wide open.

As soon as I hit the water, my excitement changed to fear. I shot down beneath the surface with a mouthful of chlorinated water. Panic suddenly gripped me as I remembered I didn't know how to swim. My lungs burned, my arms and legs flailed wildly, and I couldn't breathe. For the first time in my life, I was afraid I was going to die. My father saw me in distress and quickly pulled me to the surface. He brought me to the side of the pool where I coughed up water and gasped for air.

I didn't drown that day, but for years to come, I was afraid that I might. I refused to venture near any body of water. The sight of an ocean, pond, lake, or pool sent me into a panic and immediately brought back terrible memories of the slide. Though the pool experience lasted only a few minutes, it nearly scared me to death.

God knows fear can stop us from enjoying the life He has planned for us. This is why the Bible repeatedly tells us not to fear. Here's what it says in Isaiah 41:10. "So do not fear, for I am with you; do not be dismayed, for I am your God. I will strengthen you and help you; I will uphold you with my righteous right hand."

God is with us, even in the midst of our greatest fears. In I Samuel 17:1-51, we learn about a brave young man named David who faced a prideful giant named Goliath. When everyone else fearfully backed away from Goliath, David stepped forward to face the giant. Young David was not intimidated by or afraid of the giant because he trusted in God. David chose faith over fear and Goliath was defeated.

Take a few moments to recall your experiences with fear. Use your recollections to answer these journal questions about fear.

Parent Journal: Fear

1. Who is a brave person you admire? Why do you admire this person?

2. What physical symptoms do you experience when you are afraid?

3. When was the last time you were afraid? Describe the situation.

Parent Journal: Fear

4.   What is something you used to fear that you no longer fear?

5.   What comforts you when you are afraid? Why does this comfort you?

6.   When your child feels afraid, what can you do to comfort him or her?

Parent Journal: Fear

Prayer Requests:

I just want to say...

Child Journal: Fear

1. Who is a brave person you admire? Why do you admire this person?

2. What physical symptoms do you experience when you are afraid?

3. When was the last time you were afraid? Describe the situation.

Child Journal: Fear

4. What is something you used to fear that you no longer fear?

5. What comforts you when you are afraid? Why does this comfort you?

6. When your parent feels afraid, what can you do to comfort him or her?

Child Journal: Fear

Prayer Requests:

I just want to say...

4. Cracking Up: Laughter

My youngest daughter is six years old and she loves to tell jokes. Whenever she tells a joke, she's usually the one who laughs longest, hardest, and loudest. Her laugh is fabulously high-pitched and bubbly. And when she finds something to be exceptionally funny, that unmistakable laugh shoots from her little body just like the shaken contents of a bottled soda! Whenever my daughter launches into a laughing fit, I usually end up laughing right along with her. Laughter is contagious!

Laughter is a topic that has begun to capture the attention of scientists and psychologists. They are studying laughter in order to learn how it affects our bodies and our minds. Some of their research seems to show that when we laugh, our bodies release endorphins, natural chemicals that help us feel good. These endorphins are thought to improve our moods and help us sleep better. Early conclusions seem to show that laughter is good for us.

The benefits of laughter are not a surprise to God. After all, He's the one who created us and the laughter we enjoy. Today's researchers are just now beginning to understand what God has known all along. It's good to laugh! In Proverbs 17:22 King Solomon says, "A cheerful heart is good medicine, but a crushed spirit dries up the bones." The idea of laughter as medicine goes all the way back to ancient times. Laughter is another one of God's gifts to us.

When was the last time you had a good laugh? I'm not talking about a little giggle or a quick chuckle. I'm talking about the kind of laugh that brings tears to your eyes, makes it hard to breathe, causes your stomach muscles to ache, and maybe even forces you to snort! That's the lively laughter that works like a medicine.

If you're feeling down today, you may need a dose of funny medicine. Here's what I prescribe. Reflect upon life's funny moments by answering these journal questions.

Parent Journal: Laughter

1. What is one of the funniest things you've ever seen?

2. What is something your child does that makes you laugh?

3. Write down a joke or riddle that makes you laugh. Where did you learn this joke or riddle?

Parent Journal: Laughter

4. Name a person who can always make you laugh. Why is this person able to make you laugh?

5. What is the funniest thing that has ever happened to you?

6. Whose laugh do you most enjoy? Why do you like to hear this person laugh?

Parent Journal: Laughter

Prayer Requests:

I just want to say...

Child Journal: Laughter

1. What is one of the funniest things you've ever seen?

2. What is something your parent does that makes you laugh?

3. Write down a joke or riddle that makes you laugh. Where did you learn this joke or riddle?

Child Journal: Laughter

4. Name a person who can always make you laugh. Why is this person able to make you laugh?

5. What is the funniest thing that has ever happened to you?

6. Whose laugh do you most enjoy? Why do you like to hear this person laugh?

Child Journal: Laughter

Prayer Requests:

I just want to say...

5. Looking Ahead: The Future

Way back in the day, when I was a young girl, I owned a bright pink diary. My diary was secured with a lock and I was the only one who had the key. Several times a week, I would unlock the diary, open up to a fresh page, and write out my thoughts. These private entries included detailed paragraphs about the day's events and sometimes featured lengthy birthday wish lists. My diary was also where I recorded plans for the future.

Looking back at my early writings is pretty entertaining. According to my records, I wanted to marry a handsome man and live in a beautiful palace in the countryside. I planned to have four children, two sets of identical twins with rhyming names. I wanted to be a popular teacher who made a million dollars per year, while starring in hit movies on the weekends. At age twelve, I thought I had my future all figured out!

It turns out God's plans for my life were different than the plans I'd written down years ago. I am married to a loving and handsome man, but God knew my grass and pollen allergy issues wouldn't allow me to live comfortably in the countryside! The two sets of twins I'd imagined weren't part of God's plan either, but my three amazing daughters were. Not only were God's plans different than what I'd imagined, His plans were much better than anything I'd ever jotted down in my precious pink diary.

The Bible tells us about a girl named Mary who also had plans for her life. She was preparing to marry Joseph when an angelic messenger brought strange news to her. The angel explained that God had chosen her to carry and give birth to Jesus, God's only Son. This amazing news shocked Mary and caused her to put her personal plans on hold. Mary accepted her God given assignment and became part of the greatest story ever told!

Jeremiah, the prophet, offered encouraging words to those who follow the Lord. Jeremiah 29:11 says, "For I know the plans I have for you," declares the Lord, "plans to prosper you and not to harm you, plans to give you hope and a future." God loves us, and He always has our best interests in mind. His plans for us are awesome and they far exceed anything we could ever ask or imagine.

It's fun to think about the future and make plans for the years to come. But as we plan, we must always pray and ask God to give us direction. Over the next several days, take time to share your thoughts about the future by completing this set of journal questions.

Parent Journal: The Future

1. What is one thing you'd like to accomplish before you die? Why is this accomplishment important to you?

2. What would you like to be doing in five years?

3. What is one thing you can do right now to make your future better?

Parent Journal: The Future

4. What do you think the world will be like twenty years from now?

5. Who are the members of your future family? Think about a spouse, children, grandchildren, etc.

6. What is one piece of advice you'd give to your future self?

Parent Journal: The Future

Prayer Requests:

I just want to say...

Child Journal: The Future

1. What is one thing you'd like to accomplish before you die? Why is this accomplishment important to you?

2. What would you like to be doing in five years?

3. What is one thing you can do right now to make your future better?

Child Journal: The Future

4. What do you think the world will be like twenty years from now?

5. Who are the members of your future family? Think about a spouse, children, grandchildren, etc.

6. What is one piece of advice you'd give to your future self?

Child Journal: The Future

Prayer Requests:

I just want to say...

6. Lessons Learned: Education

We are a homeschooling family. My husband is the principal, I am the teacher, and our daughters are the students. Though we school in nearly every room of the house, my older girls often prefer to work on assignments in their quiet bedrooms. Not long ago, as I came up the steps to check on the girls' progress, I overheard one of my daughters talking to herself in frustration. "Seriously, I don't care about the discounted cost of this man's fishing gear! He needs to get a calculator. Why do I have to figure this out? I'll never use this stuff."

My daughter's words match many students' thoughts. They sometimes wonder about the importance of what they're being taught. They struggle to see how their learning connects to the real world. After all, when was the last time someone asked you to compute the square footage of the barn she was constructing? When was the last time someone planning a trip called on you to determine how fast two different trains were traveling? Not recently.

What we learn may sometimes seem disconnected or unimportant, but God never wastes a lesson. He provides unexpected opportunities for us to use what we've learned. This is exactly what happened to Paul. He is best known as the man who persecuted Christians until a dramatic encounter with Jesus changed his life forever. But Paul was also an intelligent, well-educated man and God put every bit of his learning to great use.

Paul was born into a Jewish and Roman family. He was taught by Gamaliel, one of ancient Greece's best Jewish teachers. Gamaliel taught Paul the ways of Jewish life and explained Jewish traditions. In addition, Paul's Roman citizenship gave him protection, as well as an expert understanding of Rome's customs and laws. As a young student, Paul had no idea he would use his knowledge and background to spread the gospel of Jesus Christ throughout the world. God knew it all along.

Turn to Acts 22:1-21 and read about Paul's Jewish heritage and his encounter with Jesus. Then, read Acts 22:22-29 to learn how Paul's Roman citizenship once saved him from harm. After reading, write responses to these journal prompt.

Parent Journal: Education

1. Who was your favorite teacher? Why?

2. What were your favorite and least favorite school subjects? Why?

3. What type of learner are you: visual, auditory, hands-on, or a combination? How do you know?

Parent Journal: Education

4. What is something you'd like to learn how to do? Why?

5. How have you used something you've learned to bless another person?

6. What is something you didn't want to learn but are now glad you did learn? Why?

Parent Journal: Education

Prayer Requests:

I just want to say...

Child Journal: Education

1. Who is your favorite teacher? Why?

2. What are your favorite and least favorite school subjects? Why?

3. What type of learner are you: visual, auditory, hands-on, or a combination? How do you know?

Child Journal: Education

4. What is something you'd like to learn how to do? Why?

5. How have you used something you've learned to bless another person?

6. What is something you didn't want to learn but are now glad you did learn? Why?

Prayer Requests:

I just want to say...

7. Fired Up: Anger

My daughter was making her way across the field, heading toward us. She hadn't gotten to the van yet, but I could tell she was angry. She held her soccer ball in a tight grip and her backpack unhappily flopped up and down between her shoulders. Her stiff posture, tight jaw, and rapid steps told me practice hadn't gone well. Later that night, I listened as my daughter explained what happened during those two hours.

Each of us gets angry sometimes. Anger is a natural emotion meant to encourage us, motivate us, and even protect us. But if we don't handle our anger appropriately, it can cause problems. Moses, one of the Bible's greatest leaders, learned a tough truth about what happens when someone does not control his anger.

God used Moses to lead His people, the Israelites, out of slavery. For hundreds of years the Israelites had worked in harsh conditions in Egypt. Once out of Egypt, the Israelites were on their way to the land God had promised them. But because of disobedience, the Israelites' desert journey to the Promised Land grew long and they began to grumble. They were tired. They didn't like the food. They began to think slavery in Egypt was better than traveling through the desert.

All of these complaints bothered Moses and made it hard for him to lead the Israelites. One day, the Israelites began to complain because they didn't have any water. God told Moses to gather the Israelites together in one place. Then God instructed Moses to stand before them and speak to a rock. God explained that water would pour from the rock to refresh the Israelites and their animals.

However, Moses was still angry with the complaining Israelites. Instead of speaking to the rock as God had said, Moses angrily struck the rock with his staff. Water poured from the rock, but God was displeased with Moses' angry response. As punishment for his disobedience, God did not allow Moses to enter the Promised Land. You can read the entire account in Numbers 20:1-13 and in Deuteronomy 34:1-8.

Let's be honest. Even the most calm and even-tempered person gets angry at times. That includes you and me! Think about anger and how you respond to it. Then answer these journal questions about anger.

Parent Journal: Anger

1. What is something that makes you angry? Why?

2. How do you respond when someone makes you angry?

3. Is your usual response to anger helpful or harmful? Why?

Parent Journal: Anger

4. Can getting angry be a good thing? Why or why not?

5. Describe a time when you made someone else angry.

6. Is it hard or easy for you to forgive someone who has angered or wronged you? Why or why not?

Parent Journal: Anger

Prayer Requests:

I just want to say...

Child Journal: Anger

1. What is something that makes you angry? Why?

2. How do you respond when someone makes you angry?

3. Is your usual response to anger helpful or harmful? Why?

Child Journal: Anger

4. Can getting angry be a good thing? Why or why not?

5. Describe a time when you made someone else angry.

6. Is it hard or easy for you to forgive someone who has angered or wronged you? Why or why not?

Child Journal: Anger

Prayer Requests:

I just want to say...

8. Digging In: Food

Lean in and let me share a little secret with you. I love to eat! A chocolate ice cream sundae topped with hot fudge, a huge swirl of whipped cream, and lots of sprinkles excites me. The first bite of a spicy taco makes me want to do a happy dance and eating a stack of my daughter's fluffy homemade pancakes is a yummy Saturday morning treat. It doesn't matter if the meal is breakfast, lunch, or dinner or if the dish is sweet or savory. A good meal always pleases me. Can you relate?

For me, the one thing that makes any meal better is when I can enjoy it with family and friends. It doesn't matter if we're outside on the backyard deck dishing out a homemade Sunday brunch or if we're seated at the dinner table eating a "Thank God It's Friday" pizza. My food just seems to taste better when I eat it alongside the people I love most. Delicious food and interesting conversation are a winning combination!

This mix of food and fellowship isn't a new idea. In the early years of the Christian church, the believers gathered together regularly. They shared resources and they also shared meals. Acts 2:46 tells us, "Every day they continued to meet together in the temple courts. They broke bread in their homes and ate together with glad and sincere hearts,". When these ancient believers sat down together, meals fed their bodies and Christian fellowship fed their souls. Everyone at the table was satisfied.

Eating a meal with a group of friends is great, but sharing a meal with a close friend is awesome! This is how the Bible describes what happens after someone decides to trust and depend upon Jesus. Revelation 3:20 states, "Here I am! I stand at the door and knock. If anyone hears my voice and opens the door, I will come in and eat with that person, and they with me." As we get to know Jesus better, we spend time praying and talking to Him. This is similar to the bonding that occurs between good friends who talk while sharing a meal.

Take some time to think about food and the people who join you while you eat. I suspect you've got some memories that match some of those meals. Think about these special food memories and respond to the following journal prompts. Bon appetit!

Parent Journal: Food

1. Who is the best cook you know? What makes this person's food so appealing?

2. Describe a food related memory. When was it? What happened? Who was there? What were you eating?

3. What is a food you dislike? Why do you dislike it?

Parent Journal: Food

4. Are you a skilled cook? How do you know?

5. What is your favorite restaurant? Why do you like to eat there?

6. If someone planned to serve you the perfect dinner, what would be on the menu?

Parent Journal: Food

Prayer Requests:

I just want to say...

Child Journal: Food

1. Who is the best cook you know? What makes this person's food so
    appealing?

2. Describe a food related memory. When was it? What happened? Who
    was there? What were you eating?

3. What is a food you dislike? Why do you dislike it?

Child Journal: Food

4. Are you a skilled cook? How do you know?

5. What is your favorite restaurant? Why do you like to eat there?

6. If someone planned to serve you the perfect dinner, what would be on the menu?

Child Journal: Food

Prayer Requests:

I just want to say...

9. Time Out: Relaxation

We are an active family. Our monthly calendar includes soccer games, youth group gatherings, music lessons, business trips, birthday parties, Bible studies, dinner dates, swim practices, and church services. Throughout the week, everyone has something to do or some place to go. Though these activities are important and enjoyable, we must make sure we're not overwhelmed by our family calendar. If we do become overwhelmed, parents and kids may become tired and disconnected.

God is active too. As we read Genesis 1, we discover that God created the entire world and all its inhabitants. We learn He created the day and night on day one and created the sky and sea on day two. We read about the creation of land and vegetation on day three and the creation of the sun, moon, and stars on day four. We see the formation of sea creatures and birds on day five and the formation of animals and human beings on day six.

God understands the importance of work, but He never intended for humans to work nonstop. This is why God included rest and relaxation as part of His perfect plan for our lives. God set the example for us by showing us how and when to rest. Genesis 2:2 tells us what God did after the six days of creation. By the seventh day God had finished the work he had been doing; so, on the seventh day he rested from all his work. First God worked, then He rested.

This need for rest is one reason our family looks forward to summertime Family Camp. It is the perfect time for our family to relax, reconnect, and have fun. My husband loves the thrill of zip lining, while the girls prefer water activities like canoeing and wave-cutting. I like to relax in an Adirondack chair while reading a good book and enjoying the bay view. As a family, we love singing silly camp songs, square dancing with friends, and eating s'mores around the camp fire. Family Camp is one of the best weeks of the year!

Activities and outings are fun and necessary, but relaxation is too. Regular times of relaxation refresh us and prepare us for future tasks. What does relaxation mean to you? Think about it and answer the following journal prompts.

Parent Journal: Relaxation

1. Is it hard or easy for you to relax? Why?

2. If your family's schedule is too busy, what are some things family members can do to make the schedule less hectic?

3. How do you prefer to relax after a stressful or busy day?

Parent Journal: Relaxation

4. If you could take a relaxing, two-week, all expenses paid vacation to any place in the world, where would you go? Why?

5. What relaxing activities can your family do together?

6. If a friend wanted to create a relaxation kit for you, what three items would your friend place inside the kit? Why?

Parent Journal: Relaxation

Prayer Requests:

I just want to say...

Child Journal: Relaxation

1. Is it hard or easy for you to relax? Why?

2. If your family's schedule is too busy, what are some things family members can do to make the schedule less hectic?

3. How do you prefer to relax after a stressful or busy day?

Child Journal: Relaxation

4. If you could take a relaxing, two-week, all expenses paid vacation to any place in the world, where would you go? Why?

5. What relaxing activities can your family do together?

6. If a friend wanted to create a relaxation kit for you, what three items would your friend place inside the kit? Why?

Child Journal: Relaxation

Prayer Requests:

I just want to say...

10. Nailed It: Success

A few years ago, our family started working on jigsaw puzzles. We'd dump the 750 pieces into a glass jar and begin assembling the puzzle on the living room floor. Throughout the day, family members and visitors would pull pieces from the jar hoping to add a few more pieces to the puzzle. Day by day and piece by piece, the number of pieces in the jar would shrink and the puzzle's scene would become more obvious. It was always a treat to be the one who snapped the final puzzle piece into place. Sweet success at last!

After the puzzle was completed, we'd frame it and hang the puzzle on a wall. As we passed by the framed and neatly hung puzzle, we'd sometimes stop to admire the scene. We'd also think about the time and effort it took to assemble the puzzle's most challenging sections. In the end, our struggle to arrange seventy-three, similar, blue puzzle pieces was worth it. Those pieces came together to form the puzzle's gorgeous blue sky.

The desire for success is part of the human experience. Even the men and women of the Bible worked to be successful in their tasks. This is exactly what a man named Nehemiah did. Though he had a great job working for a powerful king, Nehemiah was unhappy. He learned the protective walls of Jerusalem, the city he grew up in, were falling apart. The citizens had no protection from the intruders or attackers who wanted to take the city as their own.

Nehemiah prayed and asked God for help. God answered Nehemiah's prayer and he traveled back to Jerusalem to organize and oversee the repair of Jerusalem's crumbled walls. Under Nehemiah's leadership, the walls were rebuilt, but during the reconstruction efforts, Nehemiah faced hardships including apathy, bullying, and even death threats. Read about the opposition Nehemiah faced and how long it took to complete the wall in Nehemiah 6:1-15. To get the full story, read the entire book of Nehemiah.

Success is fantastic! When we include God in our plans, He blesses us and gives us the best type of success. God given success is true success. It makes us feel good and offers us the motivation and strength we need to tackle future challenges. Take time to answer these journal questions about success.

Parent Journal: Success

1. What is your definition of success?

2. Describe a time when you felt successful.

3. Do you think hard work always leads to success? Why or why not?

Parent Journal: Success

4. Name a successful person you know. Tell why you consider him or her to be a success.

5. What obstacles do people encounter as they pursue success? How can these obstacles be overcome?

6. Name three characteristics the world attributes to successful people. Do you agree with these markers of success? Why or why not?

Parent Journal: Success

Prayer Requests:

I just want to say...

Child Journal: Success

1. What is your definition of success?

2. Describe a time when you felt successful.

3. Do you think hard work always leads to success? Why or why not?

Child Journal: Success

4. Name a successful person you know. Tell why you consider him or her to be a success.

5. What obstacles do people encounter as they pursue success? How can these obstacles be overcome?

6. Name three characteristics the world attributes to successful people. Do you agree with these markers of success? Why or why not?

Child Journal: Success

Prayer Requests:

I just want to say

Acknowledgements

JT, only God could bring a shy guy and a chatty girl together on a unique blind date and know that date would lead to marriage and years of awesome adventures. I couldn't have asked for a better life partner! Your love, faithfulness, patience, encouragement, and prayers have helped me achieve this goal. Thanks for being such a marvelous friend and husband. You are my favorite person and I love you...dearly.

Thank heaven for little girls! Dynamic daughters, you are the remarkable trio who inspired this special project. Thank you for the heartfelt hugs, precious kisses, sincere prayers, superb suggestions, and much needed "You can do it, Mom" speeches. Continue to defy the status quo by striving to be salt and light. Carry the fire into the cold and bring God glory. I love you all!

Mom, did you ever imagine that the spunky, disorganized, and strong-willed girl you and Dad raised could get her act together long enough to write a book? Look at God! Isn't He amazing? Thank you for your calming voice and supportive words. Thank you for constantly reminding me that God is in control. My heart smiles when I think of you. Thank you for your love!

Tracy Cooper, lion chasing rocks! Thank you for being a loving friend, devoted prayer warrior, and dedicated accountability partner. Thank you for lighting motivational fires under my fanny whenever I tried to hide under thick blankets of procrastination. My project is finally done! This calls for thick celebratory slices of our favorite chocolate cake.

About the Author

Andrea Thorpe is a Christian, a wife, and a mother of three daughters. Prior to becoming a homeschooling mom, Andrea earned a Bachelor of Arts degree in English, teacher certification, and a Master's degree in Student Personnel Services. During her nine years in public education, Andrea worked as a classroom teacher and guidance counselor and was recognized as Teacher of the Year.

Andrea enjoys teaching her lively trio from the comfort of the family's New Jersey home. When not homeschooling or working at her computer, Andrea loves to hang out with family and friends, search for bargains in antique and thrift stores, work on home décor projects, and cheer loudly at her girls' soccer games.

Made in the USA
Monee, IL
05 May 2021